Treat Her Like a Truck

And Other Tips for Marital Bliss

Treat Her Like a Truck

And Other Tips for Marital Bliss

MARK GUNGOR | JENNA MC CARTHY

TREAT HER LIKE A TRUCK
(And Other Tips for Marital Bliss)
BY MARK GUNGOR AND JENNA MC CARTHY

Special thanks to Diane Brierley and Mary Seipel for their contributions.
Illustrations by Daria Tarawneh
Design by Debbie Bishop

©Copyright 2017 Mark Gungor.
All rights reserved worldwide under the Pan-American
and International Copyright Conventions.

For information, address inquiries to: info@laughyourway.com

www.markgungor.com

Scripture quotations taken from The Holy Bible, New International Version [R] NIV [R] Copyright [C] 1973, 1978, 1984, 2011 by Biblica, Inc. [TM] Used by permission. All rights reserved worldwide.

Classic truck image by CEM

Printed in China

To all the men who believe that succeeding with a woman is much more difficult than it actually is.

Treat Her Like a Truck

And Other Tips for Marital Bliss

Contents

Introduction	*iii*
Treat Her Like Your Rusty Old Truck	*1*
Treat Her Like a Sports Car	*11*
Treat Her Like the Television	*21*
Treat Her Like a Teammate	*31*
Treat Her Like Your Old Baseball Glove	*43*
Treat Her Like Your Job	*55*
Treat Her Like a Great Adventure	*65*
Treat Her Like Your Doctor	*75*
Treat Her Like a Waitress	*85*
BONUS CHAPTER! Do NOT Treat Her Like Your Brother	*95*

MARK GUNGOR | JENNA MC CARTHY

Introduction

Treat Her Like a Truck

Introduction

CONGRATULATIONS! You're now the proud owner of a book on relationships. I'll bet this has been on your wish list for years, possibly decades. Is that the sound of you tap-dancing I hear? Or was that a champagne cork popping? After all, the only thing men love even more than talking about their feelings is reading about them, am I right?

I'll be here all week!

Obviously, I jest. The fact that you've gotten to this third paragraph, frankly, could be considered one of those "everyday miracles" some folks use to prove

Treat Her Like a Truck

God exists. So, let me tell you right up front that even though this technically is a relationship book, I promise you it's unlike any other you've ever encountered—or more likely, any you've dreaded encountering. For one thing, I'm not going to give you painful exercises to perform or ask you to delve deep into your psyche/past/wallet to figure out why you're so emotionally constipated. Besides, explaining why a man is emotionally constipated is pretty easy: It's because you're a man! It's how God designed you, and I'm pretty sure he had a darned good reason for doing it that way. Likewise, he designed your wife the way she is for a reason, too, which may or may not be slightly neater, fresher-smelling and needier than you are, emotionally and conversationally.

Did God construct men craving high speeds in a car with rolled-down windows and give women blinding white knuckles and the skills to create complicated hairstyles that immediately fall apart when said window is rolled down just so we could drive each other insane until death finally separates us? No, these differences were never designed to drive us crazy. He designed us differently so we could **complement one another;** learn from and grow with; someone who makes us whole.

And then drives us nuts.

Why do we do this thing called marriage? Why are we so powerfully drawn to someone so different from ourselves, even though at times it can be so completely frustrating?

Well, beyond the obvious reason of sexual attraction, the truth is, we are better with that woman than we are without her.

The wise King Solomon once wrote:

Two are better than one,
because they have a good return for their labor:
[1] If either of them falls down,
one can help the other up.
But pity anyone who falls
and has no one to help them up.
[1] Also, if two lie down together, they will keep warm.
But how can one keep warm alone?
Though one may be overpowered,
two can defend themselves.

- Ecclesiastes 4:9-12 (NIV)

Treat Her Like a Truck

If you're like most men, you probably feel like you're a pretty good husband, all things considered. You're not perfect, but you definitely love your wife, and you're certainly committed to her. So why does it sometimes feel like you can't make her happy?

The ironic answer is, because you're married to her!

See, if you'd intended to remain a bachelor for the rest of ever, my "how to be happy" advice would be completely different. I'd tell you to go ahead and fart in the car with the windows up, drink properly chilled bottles of beer while you watch ESPN around the clock, and let your nose hairs grow down to your chin if you happen to like that look. I would give you permission to never, ever watch another chick flick as long as you live, and encourage you to drag your hamper to the curb and start leaving your dirty boxers and socks scattered about your home like confetti. But if you're reading this book (and by that, I probably mean if your wife is making you read this book), I'd bet my last nickel you're no bachelor—or if you are, you won't be one for long. No, you are half of a whole, and you've got someone else to think about now. Someone else with ideas, wants, needs, and movie preferences vastly different from your own. And it may be a fuzzy memory today, but when you stood before that altar or beside those gently lapping waves on that blinding white beach of your bride's wedding-destination dreams, you said some version of the following:

> "I promise to love, honor and cherish you in sickness and in health, for richer or for poorer, for better or for worse, till death do us part."

(YOU DID! YOU SAID THAT!)

As it turns out, till death do us part is a really looooong time—and being a loving, honoring, cherishing partner all day every day is no easy feat. In fact, by most accounts it borders on the impossible. Not to mention that living with another person (which typically means sharing the same bed, the same bathroom and the same thermostat) has been known to try even the most temperate of tempers.

If you're among the very blessed, you're not bickering about the Big Things (namely money, sex and kids) on a daily basis. Most married couples admit that more often than not they find themselves arguing about tiny, trivial matters.

Solomon also once wrote:

A quarrelsome wife is like the dripping of a leaky roof in a rainstorm.

- Proverbs 27:15 (NIV)

Granted, that was written from a man's perspective and there is conveniently no mention of the major pain in the rear that a husband can be, but the image of a dripping, leaky roof pretty much summarizes what life can be like after the "I Dos" have echoed off into the distant horizon.

I bet you'd like to plug that leak, wouldn't you? I bet you'd give up your favorite hobby for, like six months, maybe even a year, to have an air-tight wife.

Here's the thing: You can! And it's not even that hard!

You: Oh, here you go. You're going to tell me I have to change.

Me: No I'm not. I'm really, truly not.

You: Mark, I don't believe you! How can I make

my wife happy without changing? She doesn't even like me!

Of course, you're skeptical. I don't blame you, especially if you're married to a woman who occasionally or even frequently points out how miserable you make her. (All women do this, incidentally. Oh, they don't do it to be mean; they do it because they like to communicate. And they actually believe that if they tell us something they don't like about our personalities or behavior, that we'll actually change it! Bless their innocent, hopeful little hearts…) But you really can make her happy, and you can do it simply by continuing to do what you've done all along…with every other person and thing in your life.

Think about that lovely little lady you married for a minute. Sure, you love her, in the vague and all-encompassing sense of the word. You honor her (especially when she makes flank steak or doesn't turn down your request for a little morning action.) You try your best to cherish her, even when she insists on giving you a real-time play by play of her day when all you asked was how it was, and all you wanted to hear

Treat Her Like a Truck

was "great." But you know it and I know it: You don't always appreciate her—and she certainly doesn't always get the best version of you.

Don't tell her I said this, but sometimes she's sort of like that hideous recliner chair you love so much. She's comfortable, she's dependable, and you probably wouldn't even notice if somebody spilled a bowl of chili on her. (Okay, you probably would notice that...and post a picture of it on Facebook.) But in a nutshell, you mostly take her for granted.

You: You lied! You said I didn't have to change!

Me: Relax. I didn't lie. You really don't have to change.

The super-easy-secret-trick to making your wedded wife happy is to behave the way you've always behaved—around your car, your television, your tool box, even your old baseball glove. I know, you think I sound crazy right now, but that's not important. What's important is that you're reading a relationship book, and you're enjoying it, and you're going to keep reading it because you have my word that you do not have to change. All you have to do is start treating her less like your old recliner and more like some of the other things in life that you love. It really is that easy.

Let's do this.

Treat Her Like Your Rusty Old Truck

MARK GUNGOR | JENNA MC CARTHY

Treat Her Like Your Rusty Old Truck

Treat Her Like Your Rusty Old Truck

MARK GUNGOR | JENNA MC CARTHY

Treat Her Like Your Rusty Old Truck

I actually drive an old, red GMC pick-up truck. (Oh, I would like a fancy new one...but with all of my other toys, sometimes somethings gotta give, right?)

Here's the thing: I need to take really good care of that pick-up truck. I can't afford to ignore its care and upkeep or some of the other toys will have to go. And since I really enjoy the toys, I take care to see that the truck is running properly, the oil is changed, the filters are replaced, and the tires are in good order.

When I was growing up (back when the dinosaurs were still roaming the earth), people took care of EVERYTHING. It was a different age. When

Treat Her Like Your Rusty Old Truck

your shoes got worn, you'd take them in to the local cobbler for some new soles. Now we just throw them away and get new ones.

If your toaster failed, you got it repaired by the local appliance repair shop. Not anymore. Today it goes in the trash and we're off to Walmart for a replacement.

If your watch quit working, you took it to the closest horologist (It's a thing! Look it up!) so he could work his magic. Nobody does that today. You just hop on over to Amazon and order a new one.

If your sock got a hole in the toe, you knew how to darn it. Who on this glorious Earth would darn a sock in this day and age? (If you're young enough, you're probably scratching your head and going, "Wait, darn isn't a verb!")

Anybody remember life before disposable diapers? You didn't just throw away a dirty cloth diaper. You put it in a diaper pail along with all the previous dirty diapers (quite the stew, slowly brewing). Eventually you would take all those dirty diapers, rinse them out, throw them in the wash and use them again.

Most everything we had was used over and over again. Today, it gets thrown away. But not cars and trucks! Nope, too expensive. So we still give them the kind of attention we used to show to our shoes, toasters, watches and even diapers.

If there is a singular spiritual principle that can apply to cars and trucks, it is this: You will reap what you sow. Sow good care and maintenance and the vehicle will last for years. Sow neglect, and you'll end up on the side of the road waiting for a tow truck.

I never cease to be amazed by guys who are absolutely shocked when their marriage falls apart. They just assume that the relationship will always be there, whether they pay attention to it or not. For some bizarre reason, they have no forward radar when it comes to the most important relationship of their lives.

They're like the guys who complain about the lack of sex in their marriage. Many of them are the same guys who get up each morning, have nothing pleasant to say to anyone, leave the house without kissing their wives, come home without a

Treat Her Like Your Rusty Old Truck

hug, sit mutely at supper, slouch in front of the TV for three hours, then climb into bed and say, "Hey baby, let's get it on!" Then they're actually stunned and angered when their wives say, "No thanks!" But guys, you can't expect a return if you don't give. You cannot reap where you have not sown. Marriage is not a guarantee of on-demand sex, and just because she said "I do" is no guarantee it won't someday turn into "I don't". Pay attention. Be intentional. Do the required marital PRE-maintenance.

A lot of you guys take great care of your vehicles. You don't wait until you hear violent clanging coming from under the hood to get an oil change, or until one of your tires blow out on the freeway before you think to rotate the things, or even drive around for four or five years with the "check engine" light blazing. No, you get your oil changed every 3,000 miles just like your dad told you to do. You're on it with the touch-up paint when you get a nick in the paint, because everyone knows if you don't, that little chip will turn into a festering rust hole before you know it. You keep a vigilant eye on the tires and the brakes and the lights and the coolant and the washer fluid so you'll know the nanosecond any of these things needs attention. Why? Because you know that doing a little preventative maintenance now can save you untold sums of time, money and frustration down the road. You are great at taking care of things. You know you are! Well, how about applying some of that same energy towards your marriage?

One week it might be, "I'm taking you out to dinner on Friday." Yes, that's you, asking your wife out on a date. Chances are extraordinary she'll have the exact place she'd like to go in mind, but on the rare occasion she replies with "Where should we go?" you might try to think of two or three of her favorite restaurants so you can toss them back like a pro.

The next week, it could be a love note tucked somewhere for her to find later (it's worth noting that you'll get nearly as many points for "love you" scrawled on a napkin as you would if you hand-carved *War and Peace: The Marriage Version* into a million heart-shaped stones, so don't overthink it), or a wildflower plucked from the garden and placed in a vase beside her bed. Think of these tiny (and they really are tiny!) gestures as pre-maintenance for

Treat Her Like Your Rusty Old Truck

your marriage. And your marriage really needs good maintenance because sometimes the road gets really rough, like when you forget to call when you said you would, fail to notice her new haircut, completely space out her birthday or do any one of the half-million buffoon-like things husbands seem to do on a regular basis.

Just like that truck, you want your wife be around for the long haul. Believe me, some preventative marital maintenance will pay off exponentially down the metaphorical road.

Treat Her Like a Sports Car

MARK GUNGOR | JENNA MC CARTHY

Treat Her Like a Sports Car

Treat Her Like a Sports Car

Treat Her Like a Sports Car

Welcome to Chapter Two, where I'm still not asking you to change. The idea here, my fellow short-attention spanned friend, is that we're merely going to take a quick, painless, humorous look at how you already treat some of the other important things in your life and then imagine sharing some of that same energy with your wife.

After sitting down and thinking about all the things we men really get jazzed about, I realized I had to start with the clichéd sports car. Whether you have one of your own or not is irrelevant. Even if your only mode of transport is a beat up mini-van filled with so

Treat Her Like a Sports Car

many kids' toys you can't see the floor, there's not a man alive that I've ever met who hasn't fantasized, even briefly, about zipping around town in a sweet little ride. Maybe your dream machine is a '65 Shelby GT350 with a racing stripe down the hood and 15-inch Kelsey-Hayes wheels. Maybe you're more the Maserati GranTurismo type. Doesn't matter. Conjure an image of that beauty in your head. Mentally run your hand over her perfect paint job, then stick your head inside and breathe in the musky scent of leather and bliss. Imagine—truly feel it in your bones—that she's yours. You own her. You can drive her whenever you'd like. Nobody else can have her. Forever.

You're smiling like a fool right now, aren't you?

Quick: When was the last time you smiled that way thinking about your wife? Because I bet she'd give away half of her shoe collection, maybe the whole shebang, to have you feel about her the way you feel about that imaginary car.

Sad, right?

If you did have that car, your favorite way to spend a beautiful weekend day would be trotting her out for the world to see. That is, after you'd lovingly bathed her and checked all of her hoses and belts to make sure she looked and felt her absolute, perky best. Maybe you'd even give her a sexy nickname, like Sophia; something that shows you think she's frisky and fun, and makes you feel masculine and powerful at the same time.

Even if mechanical Sophia is hot off the assembly line, you could and likely would spend hours tinkering under her hood. Oh, you're not trying to fix her. You just want to see what she's made of; to understand what makes her purr. You'd spend hours getting to know her so that if some day, God forbid, something did go wrong, you'd know everything you needed to know about how to help her.

(If this were a cartoon, a giant anvil would fall on your head right now, and then I'd grab the one hand that was sticking out and help you up and dust you off.)

What the fictitious Sophia gets that your wife craves is for you to desire her—and not just sexually. The lady you married wants to feel special;

Treat Her Like a Sports Car

intriguing; exceptional. She wants your chest to puff up with pride when you take her out on the town. She wants you to get under her metaphorical hood and express an interest—even a small one would be appreciated—it is what makes her tick.

Oftentimes, after years of disappointments, offenses, mistakes and misunderstandings, desire for that girl you married can begin to dissipate. But fear not, you can get it back by understanding how you got it in the first place.

Take the sports car again—or any car really. Ever wonder why car dealers are so insistent that you "come and take a test drive today"? It is because they know something that you don't, and that is this: Desire follows attention. Whatever you pay attention to, you tend to desire. That is why they want you to sit in the car. Feel the comfort of the new seat. Breathe in the intoxicating new car smell. Take her for a spin and feel how she responds to your every touch.

What are you doing? You are paying close attention. And the more you focus your attention on the car, the more you will desire the car.

Just try this for the next 24 to 48 hours. Look at your wife. Watch her when she doesn't know you are looking at her. Observe her face as she smiles at your children. Track her movements as she floats about the kitchen. Actually focus on her words as she speaks to you. Something amazing yet very predictable will occur: Your desire for her will intensify. And somehow, she will sense it.

Life is really not as big of a mystery as we make it. Jump off a bridge and you will fall. Move an airplane at a certain speed and it will fly. Split an atom and you experience great energy release. Pay attention to your wife and you will start to desire her.

Stop paying attention and desire will wane. Refocus, and desire will flare up again, much like putting fresh logs on a dwindling fire. Look. Observe. Reflect. Listen. Watch what happens.

Try asking her this: "What's the most exciting thing that happened to you today?" Not a shocking question in and of itself, but the mere fact that you're opening yourself up to actual conversation, and without resorting to a question that requires a one-

Treat Her Like a Sports Car

word answer shows her that you're interested in how she works. It makes her feel special. It may not sound particularly romantic, but asking her about herself is like verbal roses dipped in chocolate. It's true. And you know what romance leads to, don't you?

Ahem.

Now, I'm not saying your wife is going to rip your clothes off if you ask her about her day in just the right way. But I am saying it's a worthy and necessary start if seduction happens to be on your mind. And as a fellow guy, I'm guessing it's on your mind a lot. While most of us guys wouldn't think twice about hopping into bed in the middle of a knock-down-drag-out-fight with our wives if they offered ("Who cares if I don't like you right now? I'm sure I'll like you again at some point, and sex is sex!"), our ladies don't work that way. They're not even going to think about letting us near them if they don't feel some sort of closeness, a connection.

You know what guys say to me all the time? "My wife never wants to have sex!" And do you know what women say to me all the time? "If my husband would be nicer to me, I'd have more sex with him." Of course, being a man, he replies to that with: "If she'd have more sex with me, I'd be so much nicer to her!" Seems like a reasonable proposition. Sadly, my friend, that isn't the way it works.

Try telling your boss that if he paid you more, you'd be a better worker. Of course, you might get fired. You see, in the real world, you have to be a better worker first.

Stop and think about that sports car again. The reason it sparkles and shines is for one very simple reason: You work to make it look that way. And the more you polish the finish, the more you give it your attention, the more you desire and enjoy it.

Look, you know how to value, appreciate and desire a classic sports car. Well, do the same thing for the wondrous woman you married. Take some time to get to know what's under that hood of hers. Pay attention to what really makes her engine sing. Take her out and show her to the world. You'll end up having yourself one happy wife. And you know what they say:

Happy wife, happy life.

Treat Her Like the Television

Treat Her Like the Television

Treat Her Like the Television

Treat Her Like the Television

Let's get one thing straight: I do not mean that I want you to stare at your wife for hours on end with your fingers tucked into the waistband of your tighty whities, nor am I suggesting you shout, "HEY, I'M WATCHING THAT" whenever another human being comes within a twenty-foot radius of her. The parallel I'm trying to make here is that it might be nice if you'd try, on occasion, to pay attention when there's sound coming out of her.

(I'll say that again, since we guys sometimes need a few reminders...)

I'm asking you to pay attention when there's

Treat Her Like the Television

sound coming out of her.

You: But there's sound coming out of her ALL THE TIME!

I realize it may seem that way, but it's really not. And if it is, it's merely because she's trying to get your attention. If you'd give it to her, she probably wouldn't feel the need to try so hard to get it (by emitting so many sounds)! And then maybe, just maybe, you'd be able to listen, instead of having a version of this conversation every day for the rest of eternity:

Your wife: Honey, can you stop at the dry cleaners on your way home tomorrow?

You: Sure! **Should I wear brown socks or black socks with this?**

Your wife: You won't forget?

You: Nope! **I wonder who won the game last night.**

Your wife: Want me to remind you?

You: Not necessary, I got this. **I hope it was the Celtics.**

Your wife: Okay. It's the dry cleaners on Elm Street, right next to the bank. Not our bank, but the bank your sister used to go to. Or wait, was it your mother? Ooh, I need to call your mother. I just remembered, I think it's called Bank of a Thousand Suns. Actually that might have been a book. Anyway, it's something like that. You know the one I'm talking about, right?

You: **Oh crap, that was a question and I totally forgot what we were talking about but she'll kill me if I ask her now. I think it was something about her mother. Or banks. Or socks. Shoot, shoot, shoot.** Yes dear.

[eight hours later]

Your wife: Did you get the dry cleaning?

You: Dry cleaning! That's what it was!

Your wife [steam coming out of her ears]: So no?!?

I KNOW, I KNOW.

The thing you love most about television (besides shows like *Baywatch* and *Wipeout* and basically everything on ESPN) is that you don't have

Treat Her Like the Television

to talk to it. You can just sit and zone out and tune in whenever you feel like it—or not. And, of course, let's face it: The TV has some real advantages over listening to your wife. For one, YOU get to choose just exactly what it is you want to listen to. Secondly, the TV has the wonderful option of MUTE, which I can assure you, is not an option with her.

But the point here is that you focus intentionally on what you are watching on TV, and that's what I'm trying to get you to do with her.

Think about what it looks like when you're fully engrossed in a game or a movie and someone dares to try to talk to you.

"Ah ah ah ah ah!" you cry, shaking your head back and forth, eyes glued to the screen.

"But I just —" the rude interloper tries again.

"Shh shh shh shh shh!" you shout, louder this time, finger to your lips.

"I just wanted—"

"I'M WATCHING SOMETHING HERE!" you bellow, loud enough for the guys down at the pub to hear you.

That.

That's what your wife wants.

Your rapt and undivided attention.

Not all the time, just some of the time.

In my marriage seminars, I tell men how they can earn really easy points with a woman: Simply acknowledge that you heard what she said.

Now think about that for a moment. That is really easy to do. I didn't say you have to have an opinion about what she said. I didn't say you had to come up with some witty retort to what she said. I'm not even saying you have to be genuinely interested in what she said! I am simply saying you only need to acknowledge that you heard what she said.

This is important because I think a lot of guys don't engage in conversation for one of two very basic reasons: We either have no idea what the heck she is talking about and, rather than reveal our utter and complete ignorance, we simply disconnect. Or, we have absolutely zero interest in what she is talking

Treat Her Like the Television

about. I know that sounds terrible, but it's often the plain and honest truth. That doesn't mean we don't love the woman. I love my wife dearly. There are LOTS of times, however, when I could not possibly be less interested in what she is talking about and have absolutely nothing to contribute. The good news is that I don't really need to—I simply need to let her know I heard what she said.

It's kind of like watching some science show on TV. I mean, half the time I have absolutely NO idea what they are talking about. Yet, I give the show my utmost attention. And let's be honest, if we knew we had to contribute to the show at some point or had to take a test at the end, we probably wouldn't watch it at all. The good news is that the show really doesn't care if you understand everything they are talking about—they just want you to pay attention. The more people who pay attention, the more they can charge the advertisers and the more money they make.

So, too, with your wife. When you simply acknowledge you heard what she said, it tells her that you are tuning in. And just like the advertisers, she doesn't care if you understand everything or even have that deep of an interest. She wins just because you tuned in.

Look, if there is one thing most guys are really good at, it's watching television. Take a page from your own playbook and tune her in. Let her know you are hearing what she has to say. Really focus on her.

Occasionally.

Once in a while.

Remember, when she has your attention, she feels loved. When she feels loved, she feels confident and happy. When she feels confident and happy, maybe—just maybe—she'll feel like returning the favor.

Give her your genuine, joyful attention and see what happens.

Treat Her Like a Teammate

Treat Her Like a Teammate

Treat Her Like a Teammate

Treat Her Like a Teammate

I believe that team sports as a whole are one of life's greatest teachers. Played well—and for the duration of this chapter, I'm going to give you the benefit of the doubt and assume you're a true sportsman on the field or court and not a narcissistic ninny—you learn to be gracious in both winning and losing. You learn to put what's best for the team (fun and fairness) before what's best for you personally (hogging the ball/puck/birdie and enjoying the glory of making every single shot yourself). You learn that the only thing better than having someone to celebrate with when you win is having someone who can empathize with you when you lose. If you play

Treat Her Like a Teammate

anything long enough you eventually discover the profound truth in the saying "There's no 'I' in team."

Let's say basketball's your sport. When your point guard shanks the ball, even if it turns out to be the losing shot of the championship game in overtime, do you chastise him, give him a disappointed glare or mumble under your breath "well there's a surprise"? OF COURSE YOU DON'T! You clap him on the back with a "nice try, mate," shake it off and move on. You certainly don't throw it in his face the next time you're angry ("Well, if you had made that game-winning shot of the championship game in overtime, maybe I wouldn't be so mad!") or worse, bring it up over and over and over and over at random intervals over the course of the next twenty or thirty years to remind him of his colossal failure. And why is that? Because you're smart enough to recognize and remember that you're on the same team, and that berating or belittling a teammate doesn't benefit either one of you.

I repeat: You're on the same team.

Why is it so hard for married people to remember that we're on the same team? Why do we constantly bring up bumbled plays from the past, blame our partners for our own failures, express our deep and vocal disappointment in them, put our own best interests before theirs, or otherwise display unsportsmanlike conduct at home? BECAUSE WE'RE HUMAN! We make mistakes! And most of the time, we aren't even aware that we're making them. (Because certainly, if you're setting out every day with the conscious intention of making your partner miserable, you need far more help than you're going to find in these here pages.)

Think about what outstanding teams and teammates have in common:

1. **They have a game plan.** They don't just trot out onto the field and hope to win; they talk about the specific plays they're going to use to win. They work together toward a common goal at all times. And they never, ever forget that they want the same thing.

2. **They practice.** The reason winning teams are winning teams is because they've logged a million hours on the practice

Treat Her Like a Teammate

field. They've learned how to act as one—something that takes time and effort. If you're routinely feeling out of sync with your partner, it's simply because you're routinely out of sync with your partner! Keep trying. You'll get it.

3. **They respect each other's innate abilities.** Not everyone is cut out to be quarterback. You wouldn't dream of making your five-foot-three bird-legged buddy feel bad if he couldn't play this position. Instead, you'd help him discover what he brings to the team and enable him to shine in that role. (You know you would.)

4. **They work on themselves, because they know it will make them better on the team...** whether that means working out, reading books, eating healthier or taking anger-management classes. I'm just saying.

5. **They focus on the positive.** Fixating on mistakes only increases the odds of making more, and does nothing to enhance

performance.

6. **They COMMUNICATE.** Sometimes through gestures, occasionally through words, but regardless of the delivery system, they certainly don't expect their teammates to be mind-readers. That would be crazy... right?

7. **They smack each other's butts. Well, they do!** It's a sign of affection; a symbol of just how close they are. (After all, not just anybody can smack your butt, am I right?) I'm not saying you should go around popping your woman on the backside, but physical touch is a great way to communicate your fondness for her, and to remind you both that you're the single person on the planet with this privilege.

And on that last note... It might sound particularly strange at first, but if you think about it, sports also can be a powerful metaphor for your intimate relationship with your wife. To illustrate, I'd like you to imagine this slightly-warped scenario among

Treat Her Like a Teammate

two friends:

>Bob: Want to play tennis?

>Frank: Sure!

>Bob: Great. The way I play tennis is I punch you in the face until I decide I win.

>Frank: That doesn't sound any fun at all.

>Bob: Well, it is for me.

>Frank: Oh.

>Bob: So do you want to play?

>Frank: No thank you.

>Bob: Maybe tomorrow?

>Frank: Not really.

>Bob: Next Thursday?

>Frank: Probably not.

>[three months later]

>Bob: We never play tennis.

>Frank: !!!

Just doing what YOU want to do and excluding the input and participation from the other guy is no way to play tennis.

And it is certainly no way to make love to your wife either! Just doing what makes you feel good and ignoring your wife's physical needs and desires is no way to play the game.

Here's the thing: If the other person ends up enjoying the game as much as you do, there is a high percentage chance they will want to play again. If not, they will always find excuses NOT to play with you.

I am stunned at the pathetic way so many guys approach lovemaking with their wives.

Their idea of foreplay is: "Brace yourself, woman!"

Their game plan can best be described as: "Slam, bam, thank you ma'am!"

In short, as long as they get to "score" they think it was a great game. But if your wife never gets to "score," why would she want to play again???

These poor women... Some of them rarely,

Treat Her Like a Teammate

if ever, experience an orgasm thanks to Mr. Quick's game-ending performances. Did you know the average length of a man's sexual experience in America is about 2 minutes? How pathetic is that??

2 MINUTES?!?!?!?

Seriously?????

How would you like to drop a few hundred bucks for an NFL Game ticket, go through all the effort of parking and waiting in line and then climbing the stairs to your section, work out where your seat is, and before you even sit down – GAME'S OVER! THANKS FOR COMING!!

Come on guys, be a good teammate.

- Get a game plan

- Practice together

- Respect each other's talents and abilities

- Work on yourself to become a better player

- Focus on the positive

- Communicate

- Touch her in ways that make her win as often as you do

Treat her like a true teammate and you both win, guaranteed.

Treat Her Like Your Old Baseball Glove

MARK GUNGOR | JENNA MC CARTHY

Treat Her Like Your Old Baseball Glove

Treat Her Like Your Old Baseball Glove

MARK GUNGOR | JENNA MC CARTHY

Treat Her Like Your Old Baseball Glove

It's a fact: There's nothing in the world quite like the perfectly worn, lovingly rubbed, molded-to-fit-only-you baseball glove of your youth. If you're lucky enough to still have yours, I'll bet you know where it is right this second—even if you couldn't locate your home's vacuum or hand mixer if someone paid you six figures. Think back now to when it was brand new, the day you got it, if your recollection is that keen. If you're like a lot of guys, you had a plan for breaking it in: a special oil, a certain way of tying it, or a precise number of punches into its palm. You may even have created some sort of ritual around this, because you were that devoted to your future together.

Treat Her Like Your Old Baseball Glove

Sure, you had lots of toys and tools and gadgets over the years, but most of them either broke or you naturally grew tired of them after a while. But that glove? That glove got a little bit better every time you slipped it onto your hand. I'll bet even if your fine leather friend is long-decades-gone, you can probably close your eyes and conjure up the exact smell of it—that heady mixture of sweat and neatsfoot oil and childhood dreams of Major League stardom.

Go ahead and get a crisp, clear image of that thing in your head.

Got it?

Good.

Now imagine someone just offered to trade you a brand new glove for your trusty vintage model. I'm going to guess your immediate, impassioned reply would be "HAIL NO!" even if the new one was a Nokona Bloodline or a Rawlings Gold. Why? Because the new one wouldn't have the same shape, the same smell, the same memories. It wouldn't fit you like, well, a glove! You don't love that creaky old thing for its name brand, or the fancy top stitching, or how much it cost the day you bought it. Your affection comes purely from the time you spent with it; the memories you shared. You lost some together (and you never blamed the glove, by the way), you won some together. It may be faded and misshapen today, but to you the wornness of it only adds to its unique charm. That glove is everything it is because of you. How could a new glove ever hope to compare?

By now, I'm guessing you know exactly where I'm going with this.

Your wife is that glove, buddy...only in a living, breathing form! There was a time when you fawned over her every single day. You had a plan for your amazing future together. You've been through good times and bad. That woman is everything she is because of you.

Familiarity can be a tricky thing. On the one hand, it can make you feel safe and comfortable. You can truly be yourself around her because you know her well and she knows you. You both can just be yourselves, without the airs of pretense or always having to be "on" like when you are on a first date.

Treat Her Like Your Old Baseball Glove

Let's face it, first dates can be terrifying, tense and exhausting. Loving familiarity is what allows both of you to relax and feel safe and comfortable, just like that wonderful glove.

On the other hand, however, familiarity can be a deadly poison, especially when we guys stop trying altogether. Then it becomes an elixir that slowly brings death and despair to your wife and leaves her feeling empty, lonely and unwanted. If you are not constantly reassuring her of your undying devotion, that warm familiarity can drift off into cold emotional emptiness.

I realize a lot of guys don't like to express their emotions. Their approach to marriage is, "I told you I loved you once...If anything changes, I'll let you know!!" Sadly, such an approach only sends the relationship down the road of poisonous familiarity.

Ironically, when the relationship falls apart, I have seen these very same men do everything and anything they can to try and save their marriages, but it is often too late.

George was that kind of a guy. He was definitely on the cold side of familiarity with his wife Susan. I tried everything I could to get him to toss even the smallest morsel of compassion her way, but he refused. He was a tough, stubborn man and he was positive he didn't need to change.

Miraculously, when he was served with divorce papers, there was an amazing transformation! He called me continually, often in tears, desperate to save his marriage. "I'll do anything Pastor! Anything!!" I'll never forget thinking to myself, "What an idiot. Where was all this energy and compassion earlier??" Susan is now happily remarried. Last I heard from George, he was still wallowing in a pit of disbelief and depression. Go figure.

Of course, the warm and safe familiar can be quite wonderful, particularly when it comes to the sexual part of marriage, although that's something that is not talked about nearly enough in today's culture. No, what Hollywood portrays as spectacular sex is the unfamiliar one night stand. Oooooh...how exciting! What a thrill! What passion! What energy!

What a load of crap!

Have you ever noticed how the sexual buildup

Treat Her Like Your Old Baseball Glove

on your favorite TV show between the two main characters is so extremely intense and how the season ends with them finally having a glorious, amazing, life-altering first time sexual encounter? Then, at the beginning of the next season, they finally get married in this beautiful wedding scene that is flooded with romantic imagery. Ever notice they never show them having sex again, even if the show runs for another 10 years? According to Hollywood, married sex is just too boring to portray.

The truth, however, is that first-time sex with someone whose name you can't even spell yet is pretty much awkward, embarrassing, and humiliatingly short. Every survey ever done shows that married sex is way more fun, exciting and fulfilling than the pathetic, bumbling unfamiliarity of a first-time encounter.

Yet Hollywood continues to discount married sex completely while glorifying the one night stand. And the peak of this fantastic stupidity is that the "lovers" on the screen are careful to use a condom. Yes, they have to use a condom because unfamiliar sex is not only disappointing, it can be deadly. But a condom for great sex? Seriously?!? Good grief! Sex with a condom is like trying to eat an ice cream cone with a sock on your tongue. The beauty of warm, familiar married sex is I DON'T HAVE TO WEAR A SENSATION NUMBING CONDOM!!

Hollywood has never understood the safety, satisfaction and joy of familiar, committed sex. They are more likely to do a heart-moving story about baseball and a man's love of his familiar glove. Too bad they can't make the same connection with love and sex.

And speaking of that glove, let me get back to my analogy. While your glove and your wife clearly have much in common, it's where they diverge that's critical: See, that glove doesn't need to hear that you love it as much—no, that you love it far more—than you did five or fifteen years ago. That glove doesn't care if a new model catches your eye and you give it an appreciative once-over. That glove will never, ever wonder if the memories you created, the time you invested or the sacrifices you made for one another are enough to get you through another season. The mere fact that you still have it (or wish you did) are more than enough.

Treat Her Like Your Old Baseball Glove

Your wife? Not so much.

I'll ask guys this simple question: "Does your wife know that you love her?" Every single guy, every single time, says some version of the same thing: "Yeah, sure, probably, I mean, I think so."

"How does she know?" I push.

"Well, like, I'm still here? Oh, and I told her I loved her the other day. In an email! I said, 'Can you pick up some beer on your way home? Thanks, love ya!'"

"You know that doesn't count, right?" I ask gently.

[Crickets.]

Listen, I don't care if you've been married for fifteen minutes or fifty years. Your wife deserves your unwavering, unadulterated devotion. (If for no other reason than for putting up with you!). She needs you to show her—through words and actions—that you love her more with each passing year, not less. (Not all day every day, but enough to keep her on her toes.) Because whether you like it or not, you are the man you are because of her.

Have you told her that lately? **OR EVER?**

Babe Ruth said, "Yesterday's home runs don't win today's games." The Bambino might have been talking about baseball at the time, but I think it's a pretty good metaphor for marriage, too.

Treat Her Like Your Job

MARK GUNGOR | JENNA MC CARTHY

Treat Her Like Your Job

Treat Her Like Your Job

MARK GUNGOR | JENNA MC CARTHY

Treat Her Like Your Job

I don't care if you're the CEO of a Fortune 500 company or the fry guy down at your local burger shack. If you take home any sort of monetary compensation in exchange for your time and labor, you share something critical in common with every other employee on the planet: Unless you put at least a decent amount of effort into your job, you will lose it.

That's just how it works.

Think back to the day you interviewed for your current position. Surely you groomed yourself thoroughly, put on your nicest suit or at least your best dress slacks and made sure you weren't just on

Treat Her Like Your Job

time, but early. You were polite and engaged as you and your potential boss enjoyed a lively discussion involving qualifications and expectations. He or she probably laid out the duties and responsibilities of the position at hand, and maybe tried to impress you with the benefits package. You, on the other hand, smiled warmly as you exaggerated about your skills and experience—not too much, just a little—and at some point, you were offered the job.

"You won't regret it," I'll bet you said with a twinkle in your eye as you shook your new manager's hand.

Now, there's a good chance you aren't putting interview-level attention into your appearance or your performance all day every day on the job. And that's okay; even your boss knows that's not sustainable. But you're also not showing up in your ratty boxer briefs with a five-day five o'clock shadow and telling your boss to suck it when he asks you to do the things you were hired to do, either.

Well my friend, your wife is a lot like your job: You put your best foot forward when you were trying to get her...and if you don't keep trying at least a little, there's a chance you could lose her.

If there's one thing you need to know about women, it's that they never forget anything. This comes in extremely handy for, say, birthdays and grocery shopping lists and finding your car keys/passports/reading glasses. But that same gift can smack you in the rear when it comes to the slowly dwindling effort level you're putting into your relationship with her.

See, she remembers like it was yesterday how you used to open the car door for her every single time—not just when someone was watching. She can conjure the feel of your clean-shaven face, the smell of your cologne-splashed cheeks. She recalls in vivid, kaleidoscopic detail the flowers you used to bring her, the eyes you used to make at her, the poems you used to write to her. (And if you've never written her a poem, stop reading this book and go write her a poem. It's not that hard! "Roses are read, violets are blue; I sure would love to get naked with you." Okay, not the greatest poetry, but it's good for a laugh or two.)

Treat Her Like Your Job

She wants that back. And what is "that" exactly? It's effort.

Consider this another way: Picture a recent, random interaction between the two of you—a car ride, a meal, the way you said good-night last night. Now ask yourself if you'd behaved exactly that way on your very first date, would the woman have ever in a million years agreed to go out with you again, no less marry you? I'm going to go out on limb and guess that no, she would not have.

I ask you: Does your boss have to explain to you every single day what he needs you to do? I doubt it. You know what you need to do because it's your job. And hopefully, you're smart enough to know that the employees who do their jobs cheerfully and well and without constant nagging reminders are the ones who take home the most bacon and earn the most respect.

I often tell men that what a woman truly desires is simply to feel "chosen." All of life for a woman is like the girl at the high school dance who is hoping for some boy to come and choose to dance with her. This is what lights her up when, during the dating process, you keep choosing to spend time with her. She feels special; desired. This is what her girlfriends celebrate (and envy) on her wedding day: "Hurray! She's been chosen!!"

But far too many men make this fatal mistake: They stand at the altar and when they say "I do," they think it means, "I'm done." It is as if he thinks on some very primitive level, "I've won. I've conquered. I got the girl! I can cross that off the list and move on." Then, he slowly begins to turn all of his attention to everything else in his life—his work, his buddies, video games, cars, sports, you name it. The more he turns his attention away from her, the more she pines to feel "chosen," and the disconnect between them grows like one of those sinkholes you see on the news.

The man who can regularly demonstrate to his wife that "Out of everything that exists in this whole world, I still choose you," is the man who can keep a woman crazy in love with him for a lifetime.

The good news, my friend, is that you don't need to do this all day every day, any more than you

Treat Her Like Your Job

need act like every day on the job is an interview. But if you go days, weeks, months and even years with everything in your life always being more important than her, she stops feeling safe and loved and starts to feel like an accessory instead of the main item. In short, she no longer feels chosen. Instead she feels neglected and alone—and you, my fine friend, will end up paying a very dear price.

I'd bet a pretty penny that just like you want to keep your job, you want to keep your wife. Just for fun, try seeing what happens when you start putting some professional-level effort and attention into your marriage.

Treat Her Like a Great Adventure

MARK GUNGOR | JENNA MC CARTHY

Treat Her Like a Great Adventure

Treat Her Like a Great Adventure

MARK GUNGOR | JENNA MC CARTHY

Treat Her Like a Great Adventure

Picture the following drool-worthy scenario: You're kicked back in your favorite chair (probably the ugly, threadbare brown one your wife hates and begs you to let her donate to Goodwill, but that's another book altogether) when your buddy Magellan calls you.

"Guess what?" Magellan says, breathless. "I just won a two-week all-expenses paid trip for two to Yellowstone/Yosemite/Anchorage/Australia/another dream adventure destination of your choice! Wanna go? My treat."

Your response would likely be something along the lines of, "Hell yeah!!"

Treat Her Like a Great Adventure

(I know, I know... If you are among the highly sensitive, ultra-religious, nit-picky Christians that have succeeded in becoming totally and completely culturally irrelevant, you are likely offended by the use of the word "Hell," since to your odd, pharisaical perspective, you believe the use of such a word constitutes cursing. Now, I must admit that I have never understood such thinking. Where is it written that one should not use the name of Hell in vain? I know we are not supposed to use holy things in vain, but when did Hell become holy?? I mean, WTH?!? If there is any word you would want to use in vain, it would be... well... Hell. But I digress. Back to our story...)

Your response would likely be something along the lines of, "Hell yeah!!"

You're going hiking / heli-skiing / diving / spelunking! FOR FOURTEEN DAYS! You are a brave and adventurous stud, anxious to seek thrills and take risks and boldly go where only a lucky few will ever go. Just the thought makes your adrenaline pump, doesn't it? Of course it does! Adventure is exciting! It's life-affirming! It's a break from the monotonous mundane of your everyday life; a chance to test your courage; undeniable proof that you've still got it (even if you have no idea where you left it).

For illustrative purposes, let's say Magellan's winning trip turns out to be to Fiji...and you've been to Fiji. Are you bummed about the repeat visit? Of course not! You realize that Fiji has countless, untold treasures to offer you. It's not like you could experience all of them in a single visit—or even a thousand visits. Going back will be better than going the first time in fact, because you've got at least a few insider tips—maybe you know of a great restaurant, or you met an amazing guide—that will make the journey even more enjoyable.

Even though you've already visited Fiji, you probably can't wait to tell everyone you know that you're going to Fiji! Maybe you started a Countdown to Kayaking timeline on your Facebook page, or you started shopping for gently used snorkel gear on Craigslist. Not an hour—possibly even a minute—goes by without the words Fiji, waterfall, kitesurfing or snorkeling floating through your brain. Your excitement is palpable and unwavering.

Treat Her Like a Great Adventure

Now let's create an alternate scenario: suppose Magellan's winning trip is to somewhere you've never heard of before, like Pamukkale in Turkey or the Tianzi Mountains in China. What's the first thing you're going to do when he invites you? You're going to start researching your destination! You're immediately curious about the weather, the customs, the transportation, and whether or not you'll need to purchase a bulletproof vest. In all likelihood, you will throw yourself head-first into planning this daring trip, because you're a guy, and therefore the need for exploration is in your blood.

You certainly don't just get to the adventure destination and sit on a chair. No way! You've made far too much of an investment not to take in every site that you can. It's a trip of a lifetime. No regrets! So you go out. You explore. You examine what you've researched. You eat and drink in the sights and sounds and flavors of this exotic locale. You bask in it all.

But do you know who does not get excited about these exotic, amazing world-class destinations? Usually, the people who live there.

As I have traveled the world, I never cease to be amazed by the number of "locals" who have never bothered to explore their own back yard. There are native Hawaiians who have never visited Pearl Harbor or gone to the top of one of the active volcanoes. There are people who live on the Northern Island of New Zealand who have never bothered to visit the Southern Island—one of the most stunningly beautiful places on Earth, where The *Lord of the Rings* movies were shot. There are countless Romans who have never set foot inside the Colosseum or seen firsthand the breathtaking artwork of the Vatican. How do you live in Greece and never go to the Acropolis? How can you live in China and never see the Great Wall? How can you live near the ocean and NEVER VISIT THE BEACH?!? But it happens all the time. Do you know why? Because when it's right there in your backyard, it's not exotic; it's pedestrian. Local. Commonplace. Boring. What's the big deal? It was there yesterday, it'll be there tomorrow. Cue the bored sighs.

Your wife, on the other hand, is not pedestrian, or commonplace, or boring.

Whether you've been married for five minutes

Treat Her Like a Great Adventure

or fifty years, I'll let you in on a little secret: The wonders of your wife, like Fiji's, are countless and untold. Yes, even if you have bought and sold homes together and made some new friends and traveled the world and filed tax returns and managed not to kill each other the entire time, the woman you married is a dynamic, amazing and complex creature. Have you truly explored not just her outside, but what is inside that cute little head of hers? Sadly, if you are like most men, the answer is: No.

Don't just take her for granted. Ask her questions. Explore what's behind those beautiful eyes of hers. Don't be like the locals in Green Bay who have never been to a Packer game. Don't be like the New Yorkers who have never visited the Statue of Liberty. Don't be like the folks who call San Francisco home who have never so much as stepped a toe on Alcatraz or bothered to cross the Golden Gate Bridge. Don't be a clueless "local." The girl you married is the greatest adventure of your lifetime; explore her like there's no tomorrow.

And here's the thing: Even after 50 years with her, there is still stuff to explore. Why? Because people always change. The only time you quit changing is when you are dead. (Actually, considering the gross decomposition you will experience after death, I suppose you keep changing even then!)

A final word about adventure: It can be a lot of work and there are almost always unforeseen complications. But at the end of the day, every quest you take is about pushing yourself out of your comfort zone, making memories, and reminding yourself what it feels like to be alive. Apply that robust level of passion to the exploration of your marriage. Then every day of your life will be an adventure.

Treat Her Like a Your Doctor

MARK GUNGOR | JENNA MC CARTHY

Treat Her Like Your Doctor

Treat Her Like Your Doctor

MARK GUNGOR | JENNA MC CARTHY

Treat Her Like Your Doctor

I know, I know. You do not like going to the doctor. In fact, if your wife didn't make the appointment for you, you probably wouldn't go at all. But you go because you love her, and because she'll nag you to death if you don't, and because you understand that you're a whole lot more useful to her alive than dead (life insurance payouts notwithstanding).

Let's say you've had this stabbing pain in your left side for six or seven months, and your wife makes you an appointment to see Dr. Flankenstein. Picture, if you will, the following exchange:

Dr. Flankenstein: How's it going?

Treat Her Like Your Doctor

You: Fine.

Dr. Flankenstein: What brings you in today?

You: Nothing.

Dr. Flankenstein: Great! That'll be a hundred fifty bucks. You can pay Shirley at the front desk on your way out.

First of all, your wife is going to kill you when you get home. And second of all, what pray tell is this exchange going to do for the stabbing pain in your left side? A whole lot of nothing, that's what! Which is why that scenario is ludicrous. Your doctor cannot help you without in-for-ma-tion. Nothing will ever change if you don't tell him what's bothering you.

A wise man once said, "It is the exchange of ideas and information that leads to great change." (Fine, that wise man was me just now. But that's good stuff!)

Look. I'm a man, too. Like you, I believe "great," "fine," "super," "sure," and "I guess?" are acceptable conversational contributions on occasion. But I also know that if I limited myself to only these guttural, detached exchanges with my wife, I would probably never, ever get to see her naked again.

You see, just like your doctor, your wife is there to help take care of you. It is why studies show that married men live longer than single men. (Did you know that statistically it's actually dangerous for a man to remain single? They say it is the equivalent of smoking two and a half packs of cigarettes a day! Isn't that amazing? I suppose the worst thing would be a single guy who actually does smoke two and a half packs of cigarettes a day…that dude's just a ticking time bomb!) But like your doctor, your wife cannot help you if you don't give her any insight into what is going on inside of you.

"Excuse me," you're saying, "but I'd just as soon leave that door locked for the rest of ever, thanks." After all, we're men and men don't like digging deep into our emotional souls (as opposed to women who seem to love it. "What's behind door number THREE?!?") And I'm not saying every day of your marital life needs to feature a tearful bonding session like something you'd see on Oprah. But I am saying that at least on occasion, you need to intentionally let

Treat Her Like Your Doctor

her know what you're thinking and feeling. Not just what you are struggling with in life, but your hopes, your dreams and your aspirations. She can't help you achieve what you are reaching for if you don't let her know what it is.

Can it be a bit uncomfortable? Sure. But so can a visit to the doctor. I mean, when he is holding your balls in his hands and tells you to cough...well, that is a bit creepy. (Why do they do that anyway? I suppose I could Google the answer, but I am typing this on a flight at 30,000 feet, and I really don't want the lady next to me glancing over and seeing me pull up web sites that explain the "holding of the balls.") And don't even get me started on the joys of a prostate exam! So why do we do these things? So we can live not only longer, but better.

The doc can't help if all you say to him is "great," "fine," "super," "sure," and "I guess?" and neither can she.

"But I'm a man and I shouldn't need anybody to help me!"

Actually, that is not true.

The Bible tells us that in the beginning he created Adam and put him in a glorious garden. But it didn't take long before the Almighty had the following observation:

The Lord God said, *"It is not good for the man to be alone. I will make a helper suitable for him."*

- Genesis 2:18

Yep, no sooner did God create a man when he came to the very quick conclusion, "This boy needs some help."

That is not to say men are stupid or idiots or incapable of rational thought, despite what is portrayed on TV today. When I was growing up, there were shows like *Father Knows Best* and *The Andy Griffith Show* where men were portrayed as not only wise and insightful, but also protecting and caring. Not today. Men are now portrayed as bumbling fools that are not only inferior to their wives, but to their children as well. Sad.

No, God was not saying Adam was a dork. He just quickly realized that, with the proper help, this guy was capable of doing incredible things.

Treat Her Like Your Doctor

Generally speaking, men do better when they are not alone. The great King Solomon, referred to as the wisest man to ever live, had this observation:

There was a man all alone;
he had neither son nor brother.
There was no end to his toil,
yet his eyes were not content with his wealth.
"For whom am I toiling," he asked,
"and why am I depriving myself of enjoyment?"
This too is meaningless—
a miserable business!

Two are better than one,
because they have a good return for their labor:
If either of them falls down,
one can help the other up.
But pity anyone who falls
and has no one to help them up.

-Ecclesiastes 4:8-10

From the beginning, God's plan has always been that man's greatest potential was with a wife. This often gets squelched in a man's life when he only communicates to his most important partner with "great," "fine," "super," "sure," and "I guess?".

If you keep your doctor in the dark, you will likely live a miserable, short-lived life. Despite the often experienced awkwardness, you let him in on what's going on inside of you. Want a long, great, meaningful and successful life? Treat your wife the very same way.

Treat Her Like a Waitress

MARK GUNGOR | JENNA MC CARTHY

Treat Her Like a Waitress

Treat Her Like a Waitress

Treat Her Like a Waitress

Tell me if this scenario feels vaguely familiar to you:

A couple walks into a restaurant. (We won't get into the four-hour debate involved in choosing this particular restaurant, with him suggesting 367 different eateries and her responding to each with "No, nope, ewww, oh good heavens not there. But really, anywhere is fine.") After perusing the menu for forty-seven years, finally she's ready to order.

Waitress: What can I get you folks this evening?

Him: Steak, rare, please.

Treat Her Like a Waitress

Her: I'd like the olive-stuffed-chicken but stuffed with shrimp, and instead of the sage butter I'd like that drizzled with some of the balsamic glaze from the pork loin dish, and if the chef could roll it in finely chopped macadamia nuts instead of the slivered almonds that would be great, and in place of the steamed veggies could I please have a half-order of the Caesar salad with no anchovies, no croutons, extra cheese and dressing made with the tears of virgin milkmaids on the side?

I'm not chastising her for knowing exactly what she wants and not being afraid to ask for it. But let me ask you this: Which one of the two is mostly likely to have their meal show up exactly as they ordered it? It's HIM, of course...and it's not just his direct approach working in his favor.

Men like being waited on. Even the gruffest of guys seem to turn to mush when a woman is waiting on him. It's almost as if we can't believe our good fortune: There's a woman standing before me, and she wants to know what I want, and when I tell her, she's going to turn around and go fetch it! In response to this, we turn on the charm. We smile, bat our man-lashes, ask her how her evening is going. If she shows up with the wrong dish, we certainly don't curse at her or grumble under our breaths; we simply point out the mistake and ask if she wouldn't mind rectifying it. (She hardly ever does.) At the end of the night we show our gratitude for all she's done by leaving her a nice, fat tip, even though it's certainly not mandatory, and everyone goes home happy.

Talk about a win-win!

Let me ask you: Have you ever, even once, walked into a restaurant, sat down and proceeded to ask the waitress what you felt like eating that night, or suggested she guess what you might be in the mood for? Of course you haven't, because you understand your roles completely: Her job is to listen, take notes, and deliver. Your job is to tell her what you want. Have you noticed what happens when you do your relatively simple part?

YOU GET WHAT YOU ASK FOR! NEARLY EVERY SINGLE TIME!

Isn't that just about the most magical and wondrous thing you've ever heard?

Treat Her Like a Waitress

James told the Christians of his day, "*Hey, you don't get, because you don't ask. And even when you ask you don't get, because you ask with a lousy attitude.*" – James 4:2-3

Does that sound familiar? Instead of telling our wives specifically what we want, many of us expend the majority of our energy detailing what we don't want. "You're always nagging at me about something." "We never have sex." "Why do you have to criticize everything I do?" These may all be legitimate, valid points...but not only are they offensive in the insulting sense of the word, they also put your wife on the defensive. Think about it this way: How fun would it be to go out to dinner if we all had to order by telling our waitress everything we didn't want to eat that night?

"I'll not have the kielbasa, the pizza, the Shepard's pie, some French fries, a side of flatbread, some collard greens, some lima beans, the tuna tartare, a rib-eye, anything with eggs, risotto, some salad, pie, ice cream and a popover, please." That poor waitress wouldn't last one night!

Consider the following statements, and ask

yourself if uttering any of them would cause you great physical or emotional discomfort, or even a tiny bit:

"I'm sorry you feel overwhelmed. How can I help?"

"I'd really love to make love with you tonight."

"I appreciate it when you acknowledge the things I do for you. It makes me want to do them even more."

Be clear with your waitress and ask in a nice way, and you will almost always be happy with the final result. Same is true with your wife.

And don't forget about the tip! Now, if this is your one and only visit to a certain establishment, I suppose walking out the door without leaving a tip won't have any lasting negative effect on you (although it does reveal that you are one self-centered, rude and insulting individual).

But if you want to come back again and again, you better leave a nice tip. And I've noticed something: The bigger tip I leave, the happier the wait staff is to see me again.

Treat Her Like a Waitress

One of my favorite parts of travelling in a country like Africa is tipping. I'll leave a nice $10 tip after a big meal, and stick around to watch the service staff's reactions. They light up like it's the best day they ever had! First of all, they don't get tips very often. And secondly, ten bucks in some of these countries is the equivalent of a month's wages. And the best part is that when I come back, they light up at the sight of my return. More than once, I have had wait staff literally argue about who gets to serve me. (I don't get a lot of that in the U.S. when I leave ten bucks. One the other hand, if I tipped a full month's wages here, it would undoubtedly render the same effect.)

The same principle works especially well with your wife. Oh, I don't mean tossing her a twenty at the end of your Thanksgiving feast (that would actually be highly insulting). What I mean is a little something extra; something unexpected; an unsolicited token of your affection and appreciation. Maybe some kind words. Boasting about her in front of others. A kiss and a hug as you tell her how happy she makes you. One thing is true in life: Those who leave nice tips tend to get the best service.

Communicate with her like you would to a waitress. Be clear. Be precise. Be polite. And (here's a radical idea) be nice. Be generous with unexpected "tips" and she might just light up every time she sees you.

Do Not Treat Her Like Your Brother

MARK GUNGOR | JENNA MC CARTHY

BONUS CHAPTER:
Do Not Treat Her Like Your Brother

Do Not Treat Her Like Your Brother

BONUS CHAPTER:
Do Not Treat Her Like Your Brother

Make no mistake; the Bible is big on brothers. The Apostle Paul exhorted us to be devoted to one another in brotherly-love (Romans 12:10). We're told by the Lord that we must forgive our brother his trespasses (Matthew 18:35), and that anything we do for our brothers, is the same as doing it for Him (Matthew 25:40). While God might want you to treat your wife with brotherly kindness, trust me when I tell you this: He does not want you to challenge her to a farting contest.

Do Not Treat Her Like Your Brother

Men often interact with each other in ways that are totally foreign to most women. Men insult each other. We punch each other. We point out how much the other guy sucks at sports or emphasize how little they actually know about any given subject. We also like to make remarks to our guy friends about how ugly or disgusting they may be. One of my personal favorite insult lines is to approach a friend and his wife and ask his wife in all sincerity, "Why would such a beautiful woman marry such an ugly guy?" She gushes and the friend beams with a big smile. You just complimented his wife and brilliantly slammed him. Touché!!

Yes, we tend to be pretty brutal with our guy friends. It is the language of men. And that even goes for guys we may not know all that well. But when it comes to our brothers? Forget about it. We can be barbarous, cruel, uncivilized and merciless. And that's if we're in a good mood. And, yes, we very likely would challenge each other to a farting contest. Even in the middle of Walmart.

But observe women when they get together. They complement each other. They encourage each other. They point out what is really nice about the way the other girl looks. They generally do not punch each other, embarrass each other, insult each other, mutilate, disfigure or assault each other, and they certainly do not celebrate who can generate the loudest noise while breaking wind.

I shouldn't have to say this, but I will: The language of brothers is not your wife's love language.

A woman once told me that her husband would passionately implore her to enter the bathroom and look at his poop. Not just every once in a while, but EVERY SINGLE MORNING! Apparently, he was quite proud of his consistently prolific bowels, and he wanted desperately to share the prize-winning fruits of his overly-fertile digestive system...with the love of his life. Precisely the kind of thing brothers do to each other all the time. (There is even a web site where guys can post pictures of their poop and ask others to rate their efforts on a scale of 1 to 10. I would give you the link, but some of you would immediately drop this book and look it up.)

This poor, gentle flower of a woman who had been forced to become the beholder of her husband's

Do Not Treat Her Like Your Brother

fecal discharge pleaded with me for some helpful elucidation. "What do I tell him?" she asked.

In a rare twist of events, I was momentarily speechless.

"Tell him, I'M NOT ONE OF YOUR BROTHERS!!"

Men, your wives are lovely and delicate flowers. They are sugar and spice and everything nice. They're newly-spun silk; creamery-fresh milk; a million twinkling stars in a magnificent night sky. If you're still trapping her face under the sheets and shouting "Dutch oven!" you need a good smack upside the head.

Look at how King Solomon spoke to his love:

> *How beautiful you are, my darling!*
> *Oh, how beautiful!*
> *Your eyes behind your veil are doves.*
> *Your hair is like a flock of goats*
> *descending from the hills of Gilead.*
> *Your teeth are like a flock of sheep just shorn,*
> *coming up from the washing.*
> *Each has its twin;*
> *not one of them is alone.*

Your lips are like a scarlet ribbon;
your mouth is lovely.
Your temples behind your veil
are like the halves of a pomegranate.
Your neck is like the tower of David,
built with courses of stone;
on it hang a thousand shields,
all of them shields of warriors.
Your breasts are like two fawns,
like twin fawns of a gazelle
that browse among the lilies.
Until the day breaks
and the shadows flee,
I will go to the mountain of myrrh
and to the hill of incense.
You are altogether beautiful, my darling;
there is no flaw in you.

-Song of Songs 4:1-7

NOTICE: Not a single reference to flatulence, fist-fighting or "Check out this bomb I just dropped in the john" (although comparing her locks to a flock of goats might not necessarily be your best move).

Do Not Treat Her Like Your Brother

I've just spent nine chapters in this book telling you precisely how she wants to be treated. She wants to be desired like a sports car; revered like an old baseball glove; explored like a great adventure. She does not, and never will, want to play the "pull my finger" game, watch you write your name in the snow, or smell your dirty gym socks. And for the love of all that is holy, promise me you will never, ever make her look at your poop!

She is not your buddy, she is not "one of the guys," and she is certainly not your brother.

Treat her like the feminine treasure that she is and she'll be much more likely to share her riches with you.

More Books by Mark Gungor

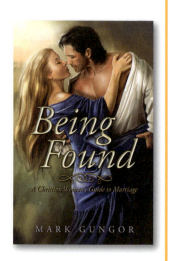
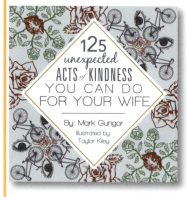
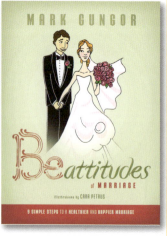

More Books by Mark Gungor

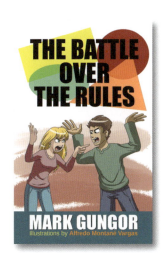

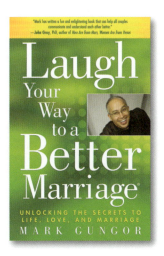

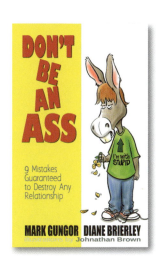

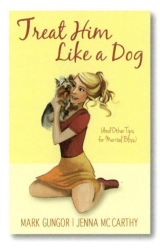

www.markgungor.com